Sensuous Desires

Sensual & Erotic Poems

By: Dornel; Phillips
A.K.A
D-Nice Keoma

Sensual & Erotic Poems

SENSUOUS DESIRES

I

Mystique

The mystique of sensual heat
Burns sheets with a beautiful feminine physique
With Shadows lying eyes could not peek, praises to the gods
Aphrodite was more than just Greek
The physical frame contains the energy of a forbidden sexuality
Revelling in the beauty of skin
Gifted by nature, so complex yet so simple
Pores, risen by touch
Imagination given a rush
Behind the different shades of lust
We seek to reach the physical embodiment of nirvana
The beauty of melanated flesh in different shades of light
Sends sensations that shines brighter than the stars at night
Giving freedom its true light

TABLE OF CONTENT

Sensuous Intentions
1-12

Sensuous Fantasies
13-26

TABLE OF CONTENT

Sensuous Love
27-40

Sensuously Erotic
41-56

INTRODUCTION

Sensuous Desires is an ode to my love for R&B music, especially the slow jams. Over the years I've often found much enjoyment listening to a good, smooth and sexy R&B song. And even with its layered musical arrangements, I'm often drawn to the lyrics. My fascination with the lyrics was one of the reasons I became a poet. Music is powerful and I found this especially true within the R&B genre. In my opinion, R&B has a special ability to convey human emotions and does so in a beautifully melodic way. Whether these emotions are of joy or pain, anger or excitement, love or loss, all are expressed through its songwriting.

Sensuous Desires takes its queue from R&B music, specifically the slow jams, the baby-makers, the songs you'd find on that lovemaking playlist. Songs that set the mood because of its musicality, and writing. I was unfortunately not blessed with the vocal abilities of my favourite R&B crooners, and to hear me sing would cause trauma to the eardrums. However, because of that love and passion, I discovered I had a connection with the written word. I was drawn to the lyric component of a song's construction. Fascinated by how songwriters would convey emotions vividly through their word choices. I began writing songs and poems patterning my writing stylistically after those R&B songwriters. I've always wanted to tell stories of love, passion and sex in the same way those songs would and poetry has allowed me to do that.

Sensuous Desires is filled with sexual innuendos, and fantasies. These tales are told from the perspective of a man professing his affection to a woman. As readers progress through each section, the level of details increases, while subtlety does the opposite. The book consummates with erotic poems which are for those who like things a little more "hardcore", subtlety is stripped away and we delve deeper into the raw "nasty" details of sex. Exploring both its pleasures and "pains".

Sensuous is defined as being *highly susceptible to influence through the senses*

Desire is defined as *to long or hope for; exhibit or to express a wish for*

Sensuous Desires could be defined, as one's hope or wishes to be pleased through their five senses.

There are four sections within this collection, with each a play on the book's title. Increasing the levels of sexual fervour as you progress. For fans of erotic poetry, you'll find that this book has something for you. This will be a good read, primed to make your imagination go wild. I hope you find your sensuous desires within these pages.

Sensuous Intentions

Poetic Conversation

I say to you I'm a poet
You want me to say somethings to show it?
Okay, okay tell me how should I start?
Do you want me to rhyme about being a romantic man?
Maybe someone to play with your heart
Hmm, tell me how should I start?
Do you want someone to play with?
Maybe, someone to take off your clothes in the dark
Tell me, so I can play the part

Told you, I'm a poet
You say you want more of my metaphors
My wordplay you've come to adore
You want me to spread my words all over you
A sample wasn't good enough, you wanted more
So I hope to spread you on the floor
Like loose sheets of papers
And brainstorm ideas on every sheet
Use my lucky pen to write
Cover you in ink, with the words I think

I, me, a poet
Girl, you want me to prove it
So I'll rhyme your body parts
Like similes in a sonnet
So I know after I'm done here
Your mind I'll surely be on it

The poet, me
You say, boy, that means you're deep
I answer, mentally I swim under shores light does not reach
So my depth is hard to see
I make use of words that'll make your body weak

Hi, I'm a poet
Now that you know this
You want me to encapsulate your thoughts with my words
Give you new types of feelings
Give you a different kind of urge
All by the structure of words, and the ways I'd used my verbs

I'm the poet
To me your body, you've surrendered
The mind was your last defender
But I break barriers
Now you want me in your interiors
Have you wetter than the great lakes
That's why I'm superior

I am a poet
But I'll need you to tell me, my part
So I can make your mind and body, the canvas
To paint this vivid art
Our conversation, this is only just the start

Pastries

Ma, you thicker than a Cinnabon
I'm trying to get all in it, hun
Warm, soft and sweet
Your pastries I'm trying to eat
You look like the type to get into fun
Thick and made of cinnamon
You make me want to put coffee in my morning rum
Maybe I meant that the other way
Seems I can't stop thinking of you since we met the other day
I'm always in need of a bae
For what I need I' ma pay
Your pastries won't one minute me

Your chocolate cake richer
Looking better than it does in your pictures
I wanted to stick my finger in your batter
It's too late for that to matter
But since I'm here, I'm gonna lick your icing off
I'm not a chef but bakers bake
Cheaper by the dozen
Wouldn't mind sharing you with my cousins
Did I mention you look tasty?

Caribbean and Indian sweets
It's because of you I'm now into these treats
You're not one to sell your goodies on the streets
Makes me more of a fiend, wanting a piece
My churro covered by you're chocolate caramel
You bake very well
I hunger for your pastries
I'm guessing you can tell
They look tasty
Can't wait to visit your bakery

I want your peach cobbler with ice cream on the side
I don't need another woman's sweet potato or pumpkin pie
Your cookies I'll swear by
I can't lie
Caught red-handed in your cookie jar
Thick
Heavy on the glaze
I bet heavenly the taste
Stuff it in my face
You're brown sugar, I've been wanting me a taste
I'll be the first in line
Waiting for that open sign
At your bakery
Can't wait to get a taste of your pastries

hick

Thick is the word that I use to describe yuh
From your lips, hips to your thighs
My eyes be on yuh
You use them to hypnotize us
You at the top and at the bottom lies us
Your thighs and butt got men like me staring
You realize so with the eyes your body you're sharing
But these playa's lines you ain't hearing

Thick is the word I use to describe yuh
Wishing I could be right there, right beside yuh
Your body has more curves than a squiggly line drawn by a pen
In my books that puts you in a category that's beyond perfect then
And I can be the perfect friend
I'll always be looking out for your curves when you bend
You got a nice shape and I'm loving that thing on the back end

Thick is the word I use to describe yuh
From the lips, hips and your thighs, uh
I'm obsessed with your size ma
By your looks
I knew there was something inside yuh
I need a word to describe yuh
Nice hips, thick thighs
Nice smile, light eyes
Cute face, slim waist
And a round behind
Your body just blew my mind
I'm being superficial, I hope you don't mind
I really would like to get to know what's going on inside your mind
But I saw you first with my eyes
Full breast
I've stumbled upon the body of a goddess
Inside, a treasure chest
Thick is the word I'll use to describe yuh
And I'm sorry
But I just can't take my eyes off yuh

Kissing Yo

You have lips
That makes me want to commit
The crime of kissing you
Your lips, words come out
But it's so hard for me to listen to
No, I'm not dissing you
It's just that all I can think about is kissing you

Your lips
Wants me to commit that crime
I'm so convince
I'm getting closer inch by inch
Your lips
So plump, more than an attractive bump
My eyes are lost upon where your lips are placed
Looking like a piece of fruit
I bet they taste just as sweet, but twice as soft
Your lips
I want to suck them off
Your lips
I'm not looking at your other body parts
Your lips topped me off
I love looking at them
And when words leave your lips
All I hear is
Kiss me

Those lips
Makes me want to commit
The crime of kissing
Your lips the flavour my tongue's been missing
You leave me no choice
Your lips so wet, so moist
Red lipstick, hmm I love your choice
I must get a kiss, know how they taste
Staring at your lips is what I've become addicted to
I can't help myself
The crime I'm going to commit
My will, I have none
I must admit
Kissing you is the only thing that will solve this
So I'm going to commit the crime of kissing you
This time, no bottle, no closet
Just me and you
I'm not just stealing one or two
I'm talking kissing you the whole night through
Kiss your lips
That's all I want to do
You kissing me
While right back I'm kissing you
While the sound of sweet music
In the background we listen to

Therapy

Turn me on like the radio
We making love
Making babies slow
We on that old school vertigo
Splash, water, falls
From the top of the tub
On your back, oil, I will rub
This house we will flood
But you don't hear me though
Pleasure is loud
I'm flooding you with sensations
Forget your dreams, fascinations
I'm a real-life dramatization
And just like dreams, I have no limitations

Hot oils, back rubs
Candle lights
Hot love
Pressure points
Pressed up against your joints
Electricity, feeling vibrations
Rose petals
Bedsheets
Red sweets
Steam
Hot kettle
Whistles
Hot stove
Producing body heat
Sweating
Tonight nobody sleeps

Sweet kisses all over your body
As body oils make it glisten
Listen
To the music created by our heavy heartbeats
Heavy breathing
For anticipation reasons
Good lovemaking is never out of season
Dimly lit room, fur rug
Specially design sofa
Roll you over
Pulling your body closer
The room filled with the essence of incense
Rediscovering our animalistic instincts
We just do, we don't overthink things

Passion fruit kisses
Strawberry embraces
Grape sensations
Mango attitudes
Cherry wine
Sugarplum lips
Topped off by whip cream

And chocolate cover fingertips
We're so damn nutritious
Hmm, yum, delicious
So us being bad for each other, I don't even trip
It's like a fruit salad whenever we come together
You keep me sane in a world filled with insanity
My love, you're my therapy

Foreplay

Excuse me while I kiss your thigh
I've been meaning to do more
But let's give this little bit a try
I like your taste
Surprised?
You and I started as individuals
Then we multiplied
Ice down your back
Cream on your stacks
You carry a lot of weight on those racks
Queen with a lot of stuff in you packed
That's what I like
I like how you do the things you do
I want you to do those things on me too

Music playing
Kisses all over our bodies
Before making love we foreplay
Don't take it too seriously baby
It's your day
Play
With your body on my lips
I love it
When you give me sensations like this

Order on The Side (Me on The Side)

Excuse me
But can I place an order, for you with some of me on the side?
I was looking at your menu
And the only thing I want is, well you
Nice and round are your thighs
I love your shape and your size
I ain't here for the food, don't want none of your fries
I want you to cover me in your special sauce
In thoughts of you, I often find myself lost
All the possibilities I've exhausted
I want to be with you, no matter what the cost is
In my bed the sheets we can just toss them
Because it's only you, I want to be covered by and get lost in

We're no longer investing in clothes
Being naked will be your new uniform
Yeah that's right tonight I'll be your customer
And good customer service is important
Placing my order for clothes to be erased
Your birthday suit should take its place
Your house special I want to get me a taste
I'll say my grace
I have a big appetite so baby, fill my plate
I leave big tips
For dessert, I want your candy lips
Like I said I appreciate good customer service
Good service by me is always rewarded
I might even record it
Memories of your exes, and your current man
From your mind, I'll have departing
Got you excited, but I'm only ordering
The meal of you I haven't even started
I'll take you to ecstasy
You don't have to say anything
I already know you want to say yes to me
All you want to do is be next to me
This has nothing to do with food
I know you're wondering what it's like to have sex with me
I can see the guilty look on your face, you want to give me a taste

So excuse me
May I have an order of you, with me on the side?
There are certain things for you only I can provide
Get you on a high
Lift you up, make you fly
I'll be your captain
Your life I've just crept in
You don't understand this state you've now slipped in
Got you feeling sensations, you never thought you could
Good
So will you fulfill the order to give your body to me?
Treat me like a good customer is suppose to be
Baby, give in to me
You know you need some of me, inside

Sexy & Sophisticated

Sexy and sophisticated
Tasting like spices, but kind of jaded
Rapid beating hearts, kind of elated
Beautiful, but kind of faded
Wanting you I never waited
First encounter, making love on kitchen counters
No arguments, there were no counters
Embroiled in lust, that was us
From dawn to dust
Beauty like that of a sunset
Passion from the onset
Worries began its on slot
Pictures telling tales of naughty mixed with nice
I'm picturing me rubbing your body down with ice
You got cakes, I' ma need a slice
It's a game and you've got me beat
Filled with sugar, about to lose my teeth
You're just right, in good light
Sexy, let's have a goodnight
Sophisticated, living the good life

You caught me by surprise
When you said I was invited to come within your chambers
As we approach the doors
You said very few had had the chance to touch
To experience being between the confines of your walls
For you see these walls weren't the type you saw with your eyes
No these walls provided feelings of experience
You were nervous, and I was hesitant
For the confines of your walls had only been breached a few times
And no one but you took up permanent residence
However, you invited me in
I guess you needed me to move around furniture
Maybe put some wallpaper on your unmarked walls
Help give you a general cleaning
This is not what you said, but generally a feeling
For you hadn't done these things in a while
It had been a while since you had company
I was surprised you'd come for me
I was surprised I was invited in
Blocked pipes
I was chosen as the plumber to get them flowing again
Unclogging tightly held tension
I had studied these walls, learned its dimensions
An architect, learning from your beautiful construction

You invited me in
Inside your chambers
Needing a complete renovation
I was the man you chose to do it
A handyman I was, I knew just what I was doing
I had the right tools, I knew where to put the right screw in
Tightness, I was able to loosen
You see this wasn't a one time job
I was not invited in just for a quote
I was hired on a full time bases
Because I knew how to knock down old walls
And add new layers to old places

Walls, walls
You have them up in many places
A shield, a barrier hiding awful faces
I drank from your faucet
While helping clean more than lost items in your closet
You invited me within your chambers
I know my job is to reconstruct them
So I'll get my hard hat on
Ready and willing to work
On walls, within your beautiful chamber

Come For Me

Baby
Come for me
I'm in need of your company
Comfort me
Touch my body
Make love to me
Love, that's the requirement
It's the luxury

Come for me
There's something about your energy
Rational thinking now seems to be the enemy
Take you on a ride
I'm beyond 2-dimensional visuals
I never had the chance to experience you in 3D
Physical

Baby
Come for me
I'll fight for you
You can count on me
You're passion, that counts for me
Desires
Comes in large amounts with me
Prophecies, sexual odysseys
All in my head, fantasies

Baby come for me
Make love to me
I want you all for me
I want you loving me
Cuffing
Winter time loving
Couldn't get enough of it
When, me, are you gonna see?

Come for me
Make love to me
No one else
Does it for me
Run to me
Be the one for me
Be my muse
I'll let work know
Broadcast my news

Come for me
Show them all
You ain't done with me
It's you I want
Come for me

Sensuous Fantasies

Candy Store

You're like cotton candy
Picture, me tasting you with my tongue
And you melting inside my mouth
A sugary treat, you know what I'm talking about
I'm there every day at your candy store
Searching every shelf, you know I love to explore
Looking to find a new treat to make me catch a cavity
And lose my teeth
Hmm, you're too sweet
You're the candy lady
My suga mama
I shouldn't be consuming so much sugar
Don't tell mama
I don't want the drama

I'll feast on your chocolate treats
Get hyper, a baby without his diaper
That's how you got me feeling
A sugar high that's got me running on the ceiling
If you didn't grant me permission to your store
Surely I would have found a way to sneak in
At your store window peeking
Metaphorically speaking

This is the way you've got me feeling Miss
I wonder if there's an afterlife
And if heavens' gonna be like this
I wouldn't mind
I already wanna spend with you all my time
I'm addicted to your sugar
You're always on my mind
I know that was a predictable line
And that's just fine
But like I said at the top
You're like cotton candy
I want to put my tongue on you
Have you melt in my mouth
For your treats I'll tell a lie
The reason why
I fiend for you like a small child does candy

Strawberry Swee

You look sweeter than a field of strawberries
Lips red, all cherries
You remind me of all berries
Looking so ripe, time to pick
You're the main ingredient, I love your cakes
I want to take a bite
I know I'll love the taste
All your berries I'm willing to eat
From your head to your toes, you look strawberry sweet
I'm all yours, throwing myself at your feet
I'll wash you off slowly, rinse and repeat
Making sure you're clean and ready
Spray some whipped cream on, light not heavy
Chocolate toppings too, if you let me
What we've started, there's no stopping
We've got to be careful not to get any on the sheets

Red dress, red cherries
Red lipstick on, hair curly, long
I've wanted you for so very long
The way I feel can't be wrong
It's just that your berries strong
You look nutritious, boo teach us
How did your body get so bootylicious?
In that dress, you're looking mighty delicious

You looking sweet is the proof
I need in my mouth, you, flavoured juice
You, I wanna taste
All your berries straight to my face
Lay back
Lift your head to the sky
As I navigate your strawberry fields
Learn how your strawberry feels
Taste
Watch me crush it
Got you gushing
Down your thighs
Your jam rushing
Into my mouth
All over my lips
Strawberry sweet

A hungry man gotta eat
And you, you're my favorite treat

Temporary Lovers

How about you and I pretend to be lovers
Get under the covers and touch one another
In places, you love being touched
And in places, you never thought you'd love so much
How about I play with your hair, run my fingers through it
This is just the first indication of how I do things
And you'll know that I know what I'm doing
This ain't about love, but a little about screwing
This is what we agreed to, we both know what we're doing
This is a lesson and today's your first day of schooling, lectures and all
It's only me and you involved, sounds kept secret by four walls
You make three phone calls to say you like it
Two out of all your friends said they wanted to try it
But no one is quite like me, and that's how we like it

My lips, all over your body's secret places
I'll use my tongue, trace it
Give you those good feelings
The type you don't wanna waste
You haven't experienced something like this
Haven't fully had a taste
Thoughts, I know you've misplaced them
Can't concentrate
Never quite had this great of a feeling
Tonight, it's our spirits we'll be healing

Let's be temporary lovers for the night
Get to the art of lovemaking
Breath taking, bed breaking
Physical attraction, physical, our actions
We're not worried about getting to know the mental parts
After tonight we're back to being beings apart

Temporary lovers
Rolling on top of bed covers
As we explore one another
For one night only
I'll take away the feeling of lonely
Hold me
Tell me all the nasty things you want to try
Tonight I'm your delivery guy
Order for me to please
I' ma give you want you need
Temporary lovers
Turn off the lights
No need to argue, no reasons to fight
Strictly love making, all through the night
Temporary lovers
Dust to dawn
Touch all the right spots, turn you on
One night only, in the morning I'll be gone
Leaving you with only sweet memories
Far beyond, your wildest dreams
I' ma make you scream

Body Symphon

A Capella
Your drums had me open
You played your solo on my trumpet
Background sounds, dripping sweat
The way that you are
The way your song moved me
The way you'd sing to me
The way our music was produced
So beautiful, sinfully
In your tribal wear
I needed direction
A lost tourist without his travel gear
I was lost in beats
Captivated by your jungle dance
I was foreign to your ways
But no less amazed
Intrinsic is your tune
No need for outside sources
Your body's a muse, it's
It's the music
I wanted in on your harmony
Your body's symphony
I wish I was your composer
But even the gods couldn't conduct
Such an amazing construct
A lost for words, tide up tongue
Your lyrics, inhaled into lungs
Got me humming, look what you've done
Your melodies, cannot be outsung
An orchestra that cannot be outdone
That's your body simply
Every instrument on you
I've played, sinfully
My lips played your horns
Gently blowing notes
While using my fingers to tickle strings
I told you, I play everything
This isn't classical music
But we produced a classic
Trust me, your body's symphony is fantastic

Technological Freak

Technological freak
In front of the computer, I've found my seat
Waiting for you to load, so we can meet
I can be your technician, your software geek
It seems like only over computers you and I meet
I don't have a problem with that
I can be electric, chic
I can be anything online your body seeks
I can be your Google, anything you want
Bring your search to me
Whenever alone, I'll keep you company
Computer love, I know what you want from me
Just type in run and start my heart for me
You can have whatever you want
Whatever you want from me

Technically, I'm a freak
I'm writing new programs
Searching for the right ones to make you peak
All from right here in front of a screen
Safely upon my seat
Logging in to your profile, baby I can't help it
I'm in love with your style
Your images got me like a fly
I'm on your wall
I'm trying to download you
No Photoshop involved
I want to print you out, and put you in a frame
High Definition, pixels very clear
CPU, the only thing I can process
Is me with you

I admit it, freaky things lets get into it
Logged into your network
I'm on your LAN, trying to expand
WAN, on the internet
The only thing I want is you
I won't browse her
Block all the pop-ups
Protect you from infections
Antivirus installed
Don't want to lose your data at all

Like your mobile device
You can take me where ever you like
Turn me on, I'll be ready on-site
Let's do whatever tonight
Taking pictures or simply notes you write
Take me to bed with you at the end of the night
Whenever you get the notion roll over and hold me like
I'm the most important thing in your life
Hold me close, hold me tight
Hold me like you'd be lost without me
Giving you light

Come Ove

You called me on the phone, saying you were home all alone
Said you wanted me there, not on the phone
Said you wanted my company
Said boy don't take your time
Hurry up, come to me
You wanted to do some fun things on top of some things
Starting in the kitchen, leading to the living room
After maybe we'll end up naked in the bathtub
Tropical bath bombs and back rubs
I'm not slow, I got the picture running through my head
Head in between your legs
Foreplay action, make me beg

Said come over, you were feeling lonely
Told me, "I got R&B on, playing those old j's"
Told me, come over
Said "Boy tonight, you can have it your way"
Told me, you had the champagne chilled
While sipping wine in anticipation
All that was missing was my participation

Called saying you needed me over
What we do, will be done over and over
All over the floors and sofa
Told me, you were lonely
Told me, you had lingerie and high heels on
Waiting for me to come peel them off
Press you up against the walls

Told me to come over
I was at work
Now I'm rushing to your place, speed limit I'm going over
When I get there I'm going to touch your body all over
Have you gripping pillows
Biting lips
Moaning and screaming all types of shit
Pleasure over flowing
Nobody but me and you knowing

You were home alone
When we last spoke was on the phone
Now I'm at your door
Planning to ring more than your doorbell
I do what I do well, your man, well
He doesn't know and you won't tell
We like taking risk, no need for hotels
You begged me to come over
Tonight, you're getting everything
I won't stop until you cum
Energizer bunny, make your clit go numb
Beat it up like a drummer on the drums, ra pum pum pum
Me coming over, is forever the secret we'll keep
Behind closed doors, we A1 type freaks
Always coming over to cum, never to sleep

Slave 4 Da Night

Turn off the lights
Surrender your rights
Tonight, I'm going to work your body like
You were my slave
And the spirituals you'll be singing after will be in my name
After me, that body of yours will never be the same
I'm gonna drive you wild, crazy
Girl I'm gonna make you insane
Whips and chains
You're gonna love me for your pleasure wrapped in the pain
Making love to your body and soul
Feeling sensations you can not control
Doing everything that comes to mind
Feeling that tingle down your spine
You on the trading block, down the line
But you can't get away, your ass is mine
Call me your master, ask me to go faster
Begging me to give you more whippings with my tongue
My name, on top of your lungs
The bed is more than a plantation
It's your body's breeding grounds

Tonight you working on body fields
Tell me you love how my body feels
Do what you need to, to please me
Be rough, I never said this shit would be easy
No need to pick cotton
Use your lips to spoil me rotten

Slave for the night
Sexual freedom is your fight
Use your imagination to fill out all the little details
Call me master D
I want you to scream
I want you to moan
I want you to bite
You'll never forget this experience
Freedom comes at the break of dawn
Bed breaking, we far beyond
Wishing I'd never let you go
Running back to me like I was your north star

Controlling every inch of your frame
Branding my name to every thought in your brain
Wild, didn't think I'd be the one
You, I've tamed
Thick, in frame
Running away ain't your end game
Turn off all the lights
Sex lasting all through the night
You will never be the same
Never thought you'd like it so much
Being whipped and chained

Your teeth are shaking
From all this ice you've been biting
Let me get up inside your mouth
Be like your dentist for the night
Except I won't use a scope
My pen is, the tool
I'll use to write the quotes
Words to speak, words you spoke
Pressed against the walls of your jaw
My pen is, the tool
That'll have you twisting your tongue
My ink all in your mouth, words spurting out

I want you to take off your drawls
Take it off, slowly
Work it out, get to know me
Show me
I want it out of your tone
I want to inject your mind with ideas
Ideas you'll eject from your mouth
Wrap your lips all around them
Your tongue, roll it off, the tip
I'm just trying to teach
And these are just a few of my tricks
I'm focusing on teaching you how to speak
Every syllable taste them
Suck on that phrase
Use your lips to press against it
Let the excess drip
All on your chin
Every Syl-La-Ble
Move your tongue up and down
Round and round
Put your lips together, make some sounds
No need to be sophisticated or tidy
You're just learning
Be as nasty as you wish
You'll only get better pitch by pitch

Let the taste stay on your tongue
Keep going
Quitting
Get the thought out of your mind
Spit if you need to
Don't let your mouth get too dry
Feel each syllable deep in your throat
Make sure you feel it there
Just don't choke too much
My pen is merely a tool
To help you find the vowels
Enjoy the taste of my ideas between your cheeks
As you pronounce
Every syllable

antasizing Passionate Desires

Thick lips, crazy eyes
Do you know what you're doing to me?
Naw, I bet you don't even realize
Let me bring that heat
As I go right in between your thighs
Got me feeling you like some warm apple pies
Devil eyes, you make me rise
And it should be no surprise
That I fantasize about exploring your body closely
I want to hold you close and stroke that body slowly
Stroke it like it's supposed to be
Because I want you close to me

Baby, you're like a drug
I take on my tongue
Move it around
I love hearing you make sounds
Pound for pound, we're like some heavyweights
Sex so good
Got you breathing heavy, wait
No rush
Hush
Slow it down
Let's just take our time
Slow it down
Change positions, realign
Beds are the regular places
But we're nothing regular, face it
Body pressed up against the wall
I see sweat from your neck
Run down your breast, and on me fall
Your ass, I grab me a handful
Damn your ass is a handful
A big ass booty
I need more than a sample

Get you soaking wet, my only endeavour
No need for games, I'm not trying to be clever
I'm just here to give your body its nightly pleasures
How ever you want it
I don't make promises
But my commitment is hard to measure
Let me be honest
I'll become the ruler of your fantasies
I want you to take off your panties, please
This is about to get serious and I've already been teased
So lay down on this bed and let me put your mind at ease
I've got a gift
Which is giving your body exactly what it needs

Complicated jesters
Got your body feeling all different kinds of pleasures
Got you hot
While your breast and nipples become so tender

I come hard, real, you know I ain't a pretender
I do as I say and a little more for safety measures

We're gonna get nasty, freaky
Just plain icky but in a sophisticated way
No clothes on cause we came here strictly to play
A game where we're always close
I'll make you feel good in the ways you'll love the most
We'll share dinner while putting up a toast
Because we both know this will be just an introduction
The segue to what we love doing most
Touching
Stroke, stroke
Now that's a good feeling dope, dope

Vivid Fantasies Ch.1 *The Dream*

The excitement of sex had her dreaming and she began to sweat
Now her bed's all wet
Her legs became tense and her lips began to shiver
Cause in her head the man of her dreams knew how to deliver
Anything her body needed
He would give her
Or so it seemed
For it's what she dreamed
Ice cubes lay upon her lover's stomach
She used her tongue to rub it, from the bottom to the top
Drinking the liquid that remains upon his body
With her ice-chilled lips
It was cold kisses around the neck and upon the chest
It was his turn now and she was excited for what he'd do next

All the while in the real world
She lies alone in her bed, sweating
In her dream
She was enjoying so much, what she was getting
Her thighs tighten and her lips she was biting
Her breast she squeezed
One hand was placed in between her thighs
Emulating the man that was only there in her mind

In her head, it was her dream lover's turn
Her body he sure loved to turn
Turned out from every direction
For his touch, she yearned
Her affection
He had earned
First, he made her stand up
Pressed her against the wall
Then slowly down her body, his lips would climb
Until her sweet juicy lady berry, he'd find
Upon discovery, he'd lift her above his shoulders
She'd wrapped her legs around his neck
While still pressed against the wall
A feast, like a king surely he did eat
The fantasy wasn't over, foreplay had just begun
And she loves to play

He then laid her down on the bed
She then reached out to grab his third leg
Then licked its tip, then slowly the rest in her mouth she slipped
She sucked it like a piece of candy that was her favourite flavours
She did it slowly, so the taste she could savour
Moaning out of control, in her real bed she's going wild
He flipped her over on her stomach
Ass arched into the air
He grabbed it and pulled her closer
And slowly started to enter from the rear
He was giving her what she wanted
Simply put he began to screw her, enter deep into her
And she felt him like he was there

Vivid Fantasies Ch.2 *Almost Rea*

Her fantasy was vivid
Sex was so good it was almost like she lived it
Because all her passion to this imaginary man she gave it
Her lips she licked it
Now her tongue to him she gives it
She's getting hot outside her dreams
So her top she lifts it, over her head
Now she's half-naked lying in her bed
No bra, topless completely exposed breast
Only panties on and they're almost certainly going to go next
But in her head, this dream goes on
He runs his tongue down her spine
Whispers in her ear "your all mine"
Ties her up sometime
That S&M shit she doesn't mind
And she pleases him too
In her fantasy the man has to be too
One way fantasy, definitely won't do
She does to him things real women do
A freak in the bedroom, in her mind to that she remains true

Vivid fantasies
Now she's taking off her panties
Slowly one leg at a time, that's how she does it in her mind
She places her fingers where she imagined him to be
Now she's leaking wet
Her pores aren't the only things that sweat
Her lady parts now running over
Bed sheets getting damped
In her mind pleasure starts to climb
And physically had to be matched

She had the help of a finger, or two
With the mind distracted the body was easily fooled
A whole body wasn't needed to be used
It was the tension in her clit that needed to be defused
Her dream man knew so much about her
He was always inside between her thighs
He brought the rain
Ended her droughts, quelled her pain
Climaxing within reach
She could feel a tingle within her legs and feet
Within her mind and upon the sheets
Her dream man had unlocked her freak
Driving her wild, he was going to take her over her sexual peak
And he wasn't even real
But he perfected the way he'd make her feel
He was her creation, so he knew what she'd like
Now more that a fantasy, but a fascination
Climaxing with him had now become a unanimous association

Vivid Fantasies Ch.3 *Climax*

The final chapter of this fantasy was upon her
Climaxing was within her reach
In anticipation, her body began to shiver
The thing that she wanted so much would soon be delivered
An eruption of sensations, the ideal situation
In her mind, this man knew all the right spots
And got to them, she didn't want him to stop
It was so good, down her face tears dropped
Every inch of her body had become tender
To the feeling that was coming on
She was ready to surrender
The feeling was coming and her breast she was touching
Not in a subtle way, she wasn't blushing
Then she moved her hand to her clit
About to explode, this was almost it
In her mind, he was working her out
She couldn't just lie there
It called for action, you get the idea

He had her sliding all over the bed
His dick the real one she had wanted it so bad
In her head, she was getting it the way she wanted
Missionary to doggy style
But in reality
The fingers played the part of his harden body part
She dreamt she felt every inch
Every nibble, every pinch

This was it
She was cumming, about to erupt, bust
Erupting like a hot spring, a geyser
Never down, her body temperature he would rise hers
A liquid erupted from her body and soak the bed
Woke her up from her fantasy
It had ended and she was sort of mad
She was shaking from the pleasure
Could barely move her legs
And she just lied there
Cracked a smile, turn over on her side
Thinking how a simple fantasy
A dream could have driven her so wild
You see it was vivid, almost like she lived it
Climaxing she felt it
She laid there and smiled
Hoping this wouldn't be the last of her vivid fantasies
Then closed her eyes and drifted back to sleep
This time no dreams just sleep
The end of her vivid dreams and Fantasies

Sensuous Love

Make Love

I want to make love to you outside in the falling rain
I want you to feel ice-chilled pleasure
Flowing all through your veins
I want to make love
And the music in the background will be all Coltrane's
I want you to feel sensations tingling all through your frame
I want thoughts of me to stick to your brain
I'm so glad that you came
Thank you for coming
I'm hoping you can come and, come again
Making you feel things, your world I want to change

I want to make love to you in a bathtub filled with champagne
You said the bubbles make you giggle
So in here, I will understand your out of control laughter
I want this to be a joyful occasion
Because of the naughty pleasures
We'll be taking part in after
I want to use my hands and rub your body down
From your head to your lips
From your breast to your hips
To the center of your thighs
To that spot that contains your lady's art
I want to touch it
Rub it
Press my lips and tongue on it
Drink your sweet nectar mixed
With champagne from it
Then work my way down to your feet

I want to make love outside in nature
Bring out what's inside, our wild nature
Your body has been nurtured
I want to make love
Oils on your body I will rub
Warm baths, or relaxing in hot tubs
Back rubs
Rose petals, covered sheets
I want to do the things you'll love
I want to suck on your breast
Smack on your ass
Lick your neck, taste your sweat
I want to hear you moan
Breathing heavy, wait
Let's take our time
Make sure the camera is aligned
Get our best angles
Every take, we're getting freaky
Making love till we get sleepy
Making love, you see we
Said nothing is off-limits
Our stories of pleasure are never of gimmicks

I want to make love in the falling rain

I want to make love where it all began
I want to make love, let the fall begin
Then we can roll around in a pile of falling leafs
In love well, I believe
I want to make love to you in nature
During all four seasons
For my own selfish reasons
I want to make love all-day
Make love all night
Make love in the dark
Make love when there's light
I love to, love you
Making love seems the right thing for you
This isn't just sex
Now
This is way more than that
We're performing acts
That'll take us to different plains of existence
Pleasures so amazing
We've run out of words just to say things

I want to make love
Love of the passionate type
On the flesh, scratch marks, and bites
Rug burns, broken lamps
You know the type
Making love so deep that our souls
Our soul comes out
Just to watch our physical selves, enjoy it
So deep
It's a spiritual experience

I want to make love
Make love
Make love
Make love
In my mind
You're the only one I want to do it with
Making love
Baby let's get to it
The best, only you and I can do it

Milk & Honey

They say the goal is to get to the land of milk and honey
I say you can do more for me than milk can honey
Open your blinds and take in this light coming from me
I can keep you warm, all you'll need is some me
You can be my promised land
And I promise ma'am to treat you that way
Whether that's as a freak or the conservative type
I'll open your heart and legs
I'm not being subtle right?
I'll give you all this, bright
We can do what you want, for as long as we both like
I've been here before
I'll be at your door, quarter to four
Expecting another session, on me, your soul to pour
Arch your back, get on all fours
You're well-produced
My mind seduced
The sweetness of your waters
I've had the pleasure of tasting
Not one drop of you am I planning on wasting
I was open, but now my emotions encased in
Your psalms

Good for me like milk
Skin smooth like silk
Perfection, the right built
Excuse my sins
You're hive I'm in
Made from flowers and diamonds
Your honey Sweeter
Golden and shining
It's got my mind in
Space
You, I want to once again taste
Honey, honey
You've made a bear of me
Fighting off other bees, climbing up your trees
Just to taste your nectar
Geez
Your nest, tightly in I'm trying to squeeze
I know we both keep each other sleepless
I've milked my wallet in the past
Trying to catch me, honies
All that left me was broke, cash dummy
But you provided me with something that was different
A presence that I thought was lost and hard to find
But I'm glad you came along, stuck to my thoughts
Made love to time
Thoughts of the one, made up my mind
Someone special like you
Make impossible things come through
I guess this is what milk and honey will do
But skip the milk
Honey, just give me, you

Champagne & Strawberries

I'm talking champagne and strawberries
I'm talking caviar
Feeding each other as we stare at the stars
I'm talking satin sheets or making love on a sandy beach
I'm talking see-through lingerie
I'm talking trips to Saint-Tropez
I'm talking about making love every minute of the day
Whether at home or away
I'm talking about with me, you having your way
I'm talking about not hiding our intentions
Everything we do will be sensuous
I'm talking moonlight strolls or you swinging on a pole
I'm talking about watching shooting stars
Or third base in the front seat of my car
I'm talking about how we can never take it to far
I'm talking about making each night the time of our lives

I'm talking champagne and strawberries
I'm talking the tingling sensation of liquid bubbles as they pop
I'm talking red fruit dipped in moulted chocolate
As the excess drips and drops
I'm talking romance in a jazz setting
I'm talking head game, sitting
I'm talking pouring champagne on your garden
I'm talking about wetting your flower
I'm talking taking deep dives in your swimming pool for hours
While taking champagne showers
I'm talking piano players and a saxophone wielded in
I'm talking about you thinking about your wedding
I'm talking about me, how you let in

I'm talking champagne and strawberries
I'm talking you laying down, while covered by all berries
I'm talking about your sweetness coming from more than one cherry
I'm talking bed sheets stained
From champagne and chocolate-covered strawberries
I'm saying let's make love for longer than the 28 days of February
Till we're dead and buried because it's you I'm feenin to marry
I'm talking about you
I'm talking about me
I'm talking about all that we can be
I'm talking
But here's a glass of champagne
One for you, one for me, with chocolate on strawberries
Where we go from here, well I don't give a damn
Let those bubbles rub your sensations, free the genie from its lamp
I've got a few wishes I'm hoping you can grant

Phillips

The name is Phillips and I'm intrigued by your lips
As I place my hands gently upon your hips
I can see that you're thirsty
You want a drink of me
Well, baby help yourself, take a few sips
Drinks on me baby, no tips
As you carry the weight of my name, heavy in your thoughts
In mental visions with me, you're often lost
And the only thing that rolls out of your lungs
Onto your tongue, is my name
Since that day I whispered it in your ear
You've been wishing I was one of your bedroom pillows
Baby when you say the name Phillips
I see the quiver on your lips
I see your passion and it's so thick
I can tell that you want me, I've got you so whipped
You do a striptease for me as you slowly unzip

Yes the name is Phillips
However with the first name there's a D involved
And that's exactly what you're going to get
All night till the break of dawn, I'm going to make you sweat
But there's only one spot I'm interested in getting wet
So there's no need for waiting, baby get your body set
So say my name, even though it's my last
Say it slow, no need to move too fast
We're going to make this moment last
Say it so your neighbours know your man came
Say it so they know I don't play no damn games
Say my name Phillips through wet lips
While your body gets hot and your sweat drips
Slow down catch your breath
Grab the headboard get yourself a firm grip
Because we're about to break the bed
Already inside your head

Screaming my name
In-between the moaning, biting and riding
I'll bring the freak in you out of hiding
Say my name
Scream it loud till your lungs burst
Scream it loud don't bite your tongue, curse
Nobody has put it on you like me, not even the first
I'd say I'll do it gently
But I'm not going to lie
I want to make you cry
Tomorrow you're going to need a nurse
Say my last name
But in the morning it'll be the first, that you'll tell your friends
"Dornel showed me just how good my body works"
"Made my booty twerk"
"He put it on me, that's right can't move, my body hurts"
Yes the name is Phillips and all I want to do is feel your lips
With arms wrapped firmly around your hips

Like this foreign place we're in
Let me explore your regions
Let me discover your tourist attractions
Let me explore your highways
Study your roads
Every curve, every bent
Let me give your population of one
A visitor for the night
Let me go deep into your deepest valleys
Let me climb your mountain tops
Help me get you to your highest peak
Let me take you higher than anyone did before
Let me go where others have never before explored
I'd like to explore your rain forest
Release your inner beast
Release your passions upon me
Let me develop you
Let me build you up
Let's make a skyline
I would like to dive deep beneath your shorelines
Let me bathe in your lakes
Diving deeper and deeper into your waters
There's so much underneath there that needs to be seen
Queen, Your body is like this foreign place we're in
So many places I haven't been
On you, there are so many places I haven't seen
I've forever dreamt of exploring them with you
Take me on this tour and
Let me explore all your regions
Let me battle your elements
Let me take a ride on your hillsides
Navigating every turn, every curve
Ooh, baby
It's your body I want to learn

Let me explore
Grant me access to your temple
As you then pull everything to the floor
Sending tingles through your clothes straight to your toes
Making passionate sounds
Breaking dishes
Ready to give your body everything you've been wishing
Get you in good physical condition
Baby, choose your positions
We'll make the earth shake
Girl, let's make some earthquakes

Let me explore it all
At night when you're awake sweating
It's me who you call
Secrets kept by bedroom walls
You screaming my name, scratching my back
Baby, I know you love it when I make you do shit like that
Grabbing your hair, flipping you on your back

You squeeze the pillow, clench the sheets
I'll make you feel good
From your head right down to your feet
Every night you'll feel good right before you sleep
That's a promise to you I plan to keep

Let me explore more, your body let me know more
Girl, I want to rock your world
Find all your hidden treasures
Nobody else measures, up
Let me be your body's tourist
Take me on a tour let me explore
But after I'm done my expedition
You won't let me leave
But don't get worried baby
My job is to always leave you pleased
So let me do to your body all the things it fully needs

Your Medicine

I'm not a thug or nothing
But let me be your midnight defender
I promise I'll do it nice and slow
Just like Teddy Pender
Baby tonight, your body surrender
Because I'll render your body weak
And I've said this before
But baby you ain't gonna wanna speak
Let me take you to new highs
Baby you ain't gonna wanna peak
Got you feeling so good, makes you wanna freak
Baby, I'll make you a little freak
A true lady within these sheets

Baby, I'm not a fighter
But what we're about to do
Is going to seem like a boxing match
A 12 round fight, ain't no stopping that
Girl, you love it
How I do it
That's why you keep co co co co coming back
Didn't know it could be done like that
Can't keep yourself intact
As soon as you see me, clothes detach from your frame
I can already hear your body calling my name
Because your ex couldn't do it like me
Hold up, hold on, what's his name?
The way I put it on you gives you amnesia
Sex so good, I'm giving your body seizures
Daydreaming of me in corners hoping nobody sees yuh
Because before me I can guarantee
Ain't another man ever pleased yuh
Let me do that thing with my tongue
You know you love it when I tease yuh

Baby take me in your medicine
The prescription to that addiction
Your habit of me
The description of that depiction that affects your every decision
Love, a heart incision
Exotic baby, you must be Egyptian
Because you're the queen of my Nile
So let me see that pretty smile
You're a true work of art, incomplete before me
Let me get my paintbrush, girl tell me where to start

I don't want to come off as full of myself
Boosting my skills
But girl I know you'll never forget those late-night thrills
Had you flying, angel wings
You might be heaven-sent
But take me in
Your medicine
Make you feel like no other man ever, ever will

Lust

They say beauty is in the eye of the beholder
And you're a beauty so I would love to hold yuh
With the body of a goddess
Your scent, ooh your scent
It's as sweet as cherry blossoms
Your kisses are so sweet, so delicious
They're my special treats
I'm always trying to steal myself a piece
And when I'm hungry
I like to feed myself
Because with me there's no need for you to please yourself
Not taking only a kiss, but
Getting a taste of that sweet candy treat, your body
Just the thought of it, makes me reminisce about
Moving my hands all over your masterpiece
You're an angel
Fell right out of heaven
And into my life, into my head
You knocked me down right into your bed
Whoever created your body was a mastermind
Because all you've done is master mine

Thinking about the things
The things I want to do to you
Hoping they are new for you
Things that'll make you moan
Scream out my name
Turn off your phone
Touch your tender zones
I'm picking my spots
Making you hot
Taking you to new highs
Have you feeling like you can fly
Got you on cloud 9, way up in the sky
Come on girl, don't be shy
Give me a reply
Come hop on this ride
No seatbelts, safety I'll provide
I'll make your body weak
Unable to touch the ground, shaky feet
After we finish, unable to speak
Twelve rounds of sliding all over satin sheets
Take you to places
No man has ever helped you reach

Your body is my canvas
My hands, the brush
And like any true artist
Attention to detail is a must
So no part of your womanhood
Will be left untouched
Hush
I just want to touch
Am I making you blush?

We're going to take it slow
No need to rush
We're not stopping
Till the neighbours come knocking
Panties drop 'em
The bed rocking
Yea they'll get mad
From the noise, we'll be making
Hating they can't see your ass naked
Love, they're not making
Our joy they're trying to take it
Because their love didn't make it
We don't have to fuss
The night will be filled with lust
An evening just for us

Your body is an island
Tonight I'll be your explorer
Before me, you'd been lost
I'll help rediscover all your hidden places
And in one night
All the forbidden phases
Lust
This is only the start for us

Wax

You stay lit
Flickering like a candle wig
Burning fingertips
When you're hot, your wax will drip
All over the saucer on which you sit
Burning all through the night
A sensual aroma in the room starts to arise
I 'ma blow you out
And reshape you from your liquid form
Making you more than you were before
Inserting a new wig
I know candle makers like me
To you have been elusive
But the truth is
The heat I give will have you feeling
You can never be hard wax again
So spread yourself on my saucer
And indulge yourself with my temperate flames

Writing

Laid out sheets
Wrote one word, and
Repeated it on every sheet
It's meaning was of something unique
But expectations were not always met
After writing chapters on this verb
We exchanged words
They rolled from your tongue to mine
Actions that involved our body and minds
Lips and spines
Spirit of a different kind
All we needed was a little bit of time, time, time
Writing materials and rulers
But we're always out of line

We wrote
This word came to us naturally
Didn't need to think
Into action, we slipped
Clothes were stripped away, into sheets
We drift
Ink-less
Words came naturally, think less
Writing purely off of instinct
Tangle feet held loose sheets
Our writing style, unique
The more we wrote the greater the masterpiece

We met on Tuesday, on Thursday we wrote a best seller
Addicted to my pen, rated our work together a ten
Made you scream, wasn't expecting a thriller
Our tale had a lot of meat, left out the space fillers
Your womanhood, killed her
Film Noir, a Hollywood filter
Your world now off kilter
Binded us to sheets
Literary freaks, writing
On beds, kitchen floors, parking lots, at your front door
Every place we wrote, needed an encore
An encyclopedia of our work
Took our time, wrote on every beach
We never sleep
Too caught up writing this word, on every street

Entitled our work this word
Whose pleasures we know much of
But its truth we rarely speak
Sex
Everything should and will be taken out of context
Did it slow, prolonged our little contest
On every best-sellers' list

Trying to figure out
What position I'll finally get you to peak?

Thigh Meat

I'd love to get a taste of your thigh meat
In between where your thighs meet
Tide sheets
Tied sheets
Keeps wrists and palms close to bed frames
All in your head
You know what getting head gains
All night we can play these bed games
True to my vision
I see you clearer than a 4K television
I'll keep you in good condition
We break the rules, don't follow traditions
Your essence upon my lips
Tasting every drop of you, I can never sip
Pulling you closer, hands on hips
Firm, tight grip
After it's all said and done
Graced by a kiss with tongue
Out of breath, removed air from the lungs

Close your eyes
Can I take you on a journey?
As we reminisce
The question turns out to be
Do I make you horny?
Can I once again visit where heaven is?
Sip on some Remy and enjoy the morning mist
Sex with you is more than just a moment
It's an experience that needs to be relived
More than just a feeling to each other we give
Forever nasty, and classy
On your ass is where my hands be
Space to grow is what the offer is
I know it is, what it is
No sideways, no sidetracks
No new secrets having a major impact
Like an asteroid crashing down
Bad about you
I never want to think that
On my chest, you're the ink that
That's never being erased
I just hope you'll always be worthy of my praise

Sensuously Erotic
(xXx)

Lemy

Lemy rub on your ass
And suck on your small titties
Listen!
Your body, I want you to gimme
Gimme time, gimme space
Gimme a chance to rearrange your insides
That thing between your thick thighs
I wanna taste
Slowly, this ain't a race
I wanna see a smile upon your face
Getting nasty, sorry no time for grace
Lemme eat, a hungry man loves to feast
Promise to have you sky walking
Next morning, you and your girls talking
I know that this doesn't happen often
So would you please?
Lemy?!

SEX (Telling)

Let me tell, let me tell, let me tell
The story I was telling
I open your legs, and my third leg started swelling
Then into your ocean, I just fell in
Your water warm, sweet and compelling
Sweet was the feeling, this is what really to you I'm telling
I was kissing your neck, while your sweet aroma I was smelling
A trance of pleasure with you, I was totally dwelling
To show your enjoyment and satisfaction you were yelling
As I dug, swam deeper into oceans, your liquids I was well in
I hope you understand the narrative to this story to you I'm telling
The motion and action intensified as our bodies started gelling
You bit my lips as we kiss while locking me in tight with your legs
While looking at your reflection on the ceiling
Good morning babe, I whispered in your ear
As we performed our sexual healing
My lips and tongue all over your body you were feeling
Releasing the tension your body's concealing
A piece of fruit, I was trying to get to the good parts so I started peeling
You've got to understand what I'm telling
Climaxing, it's a slow sweet motion you make
The instant before cumming
And I love how down your inner thighs it slowly starts running
The dream to you is what I'm selling
I wish this was daily, but it isn't
So that's why when I see you, baby
I've got to swim in your ocean
Unleash bottled up emotions
Get that bed rocking, the motion
Of sex
Filling you with dick and devotion
I hope you now understand the story to you I was telling
I didn't just trip for you, I completely fell in
Sex
I hope this narrative was compelling
For this story, I was tell, tell, telling

Left To Right

I'm looking to be introduced to your left breast
In hopes that maybe it'll introduce me to the right
And the three of us can play all through the night
We can do whatever it is you like
I'd lick both the left and the right
Maybe give both of them gentle bites
It's whatever you want
It's whatever feels right
And maybe after being introduced to your right breast
I can be introduced to your stomach
Slowly I'd work my way down
Maybe I could kiss your body all over, every inch
Stick my tongue into your belly button
Whisper in your ears sweet nothings
Whatever you want Miss, we can do
My goal is only to please you

Maybe I could move my lips from your stomach
Slide right to the left side of your inner thigh
Kissing, and licking until you start leaking
You grabbing my head
Because it's the lips between your legs you want me to be kissing
I'll get to know the left side so well
It wouldn't be fair if I didn't meet the right
It wouldn't be fair not to suck on it and bite, not heavy, but light
So after teasing both sides of your inner thighs
It's only fair that your pussy be touched, sucked, licked, and squeezed
Only fair after how I had you teased
Licking, sucking
Sticking my fingers in like I'm searching for treasure
I' ma do things to make you feel out of this world pleasures
I'll treat each part of your body fairly
Use my lips make sure you can hear everything I do, clearly

Maybe after using my lips
I can introduce you to my dick
Excuse my language but every inch into your pussy I want to stick
Because after kissing your curves it's quite stiff
See baby, I'm talking about us fucking
Making love in ways you never did before
I want to make you scream, beg me for more, more
I'll have your body quivering, shivering
Yeah that's the amount of pleasure I'm delivering

So can I be introduced to your left breast
And maybe then to the right, how about you let me
I promise I will bite and you might like
Us going at it all night
I can do it with my arms tided
Hop on this damn ride
I'll do you as you should be, you know, right
Let's start by introducing my lips to yours
Let sparks ignite the actions that'll set this passion ablaze
In a sexual flame, I plan to leave you amazed

Oral Sex

I want to give you orgasms
Full body spasms
If I put my tongue on you, you'll have em'
This is an oral tradition
Work you out, get you in good physical condition
In these types of situations
I want to give you all the sensations
Body feeling melodic vibrations
When I say my girl
I'm talking a different type of temptations

From your breast to your stomach
To your vagina and your inner thighs
I see the shock in your eyes
To that booty on the other side
All over your body, you'll feel me
Make you feel things, you never thought you could
I' ma make impossible possible

Pressure building, you're almost at your breaking point
Pleasure, make you skeet
You a freak
Release your nectar upon these sheets
Got you shaking unable to speak
I want to show you what I've learned from Nityama
Pleasure, that'll make you want to slap your mama
I'm not even going to touch you with my hands
Spiritually, you'll be feenin' for this energy
Damn
I'm just trying to break through your energy fields
Make you understand how good this energy feels

Not only with your body, between your ears too
I'll make you horny from the things you hear through, boo
Introduce you to your triggers that you've been unaware
I' ma teach yuh, make these things all-clear
Foreplay is a must before I tap that ass
I'm talking about giving you a mental feature
I'm talking about laying out words of my action plan orally
Predicting futures
My tutorials will be on the direction I'll move my tongue
Left, right, up, down, round and round
You know I'm a bad boy
The way I make you anticipate the situation
I'll become your favourite tune, on your lips always humming
Heart rate rising, it's drumming
I want to lick on your ego, get you soaring like a bald eagle
I want to perform on you oral sex
I want your body dripping sweat
I want your clitoris to be throbbing quite vigorous
Nasty themes flowing all through your dreams
Now
Hands on breast squeeze
Vulnerable, your body is now sensitive

Each kiss on the neck, you'll moan those uncontrollable "Yes"
I want to perform on you sexual things, orally
I want you to get it in your head
Thoughts of me giving you head
Thoughts of my head between your legs
You moaning for all this love jones n'
You'll see me feast on your deeds
Relax and let my tongue squeeze on your clit with all that spit
Hit your spot
Make you squirt
You know my mind is filled with dirt
I plan to work you out make your body hurt

I might make you tap out
Call a time out
While we're playing
I'll make you cum is what I'm saying
It's my end game
You're thick, but you've got a thin frame
But I love how that ass looks in those tight jeans
I haven't even touched you yet
Just from an oral montage
I know you're wet
Excited for what you're gonna get
High, purely off of my wordplay
I need to see you in the suit you wore on your birth day
Yes, Naked
I'm talking my shit
Getting you high for my deliberation
Tonight your pussy, liberation

I want to give you oral sex
Mentally I'll put you in bondage
All with my devilish tongue
Like T-Pain I' ma get you sprung

Let's have intercourse
No, I'm not talking about making love
And I mean more than just fucking
I'm talking my dick in your vagina
I'm talking handcuffs, blindfold
While I pull your hair while behind yuh
I'm talking hot wax on your spine
I'm talking champagne glasses stain with red lipstick and wine

I'm saying let's engage in the pleasures of our flesh
I'm talking intercourse
I'm not talking about entering with force
Unless you ask me too
Your ass got to be healthy too
Your ass, with these hands, no telling what they'll help me do
I'm talking intercourse, fucking or whatever you want to call it
I'm talking about forgetting the taboos
I'm talking about exploring both our sexual fantasies
Shh! take off those panties, please
You're wet and it's not from water or sweat
But from me sending sensations to your clitoris
Your boy may mess around and get up all in your uterus
Shit is old to me, but It'll be new for us
My tongue on you, tasting your fruits of lust

I'm talking about intercourse
Sex if you will
I'm talking about both our bodies leaking shit
Like the tap done run over and spilled
I'm talking about giving in to the urge if you will
Yes, I'm talking about dick and vagina
I'm talking about my dick being inside yuh
I'm talking about using my tongue to massage your body and clit
I'm talking that nasty, freaky shit
I'm talking about me freaking it
Frequently
I'm talking that shit, flexing my pose
And in some of your minds
You're wondering if I can do to you what I propose

Well I'm right here, right here
If you seek to see proof
To know if what I say is truf
All you gotta do is ask

Simply Sex

Let me squeeze on your breast
Lift up your dress
Tonight we're gonna make this house a mess
Noise making, baby lets
Body, working sideways
My tongue running all over that shy place, tasty
Baby, I love that you don`t just lay there
I`m getting ideas
Right now I'm giving you visions
Cameras on, turn on the television
You can see yourself
Mastering your favourite positions

You're exotic, baby you spicy
I enjoy tasting what I see
Sweet, Hi-C
You're fire, yet so cool
Icy
Your body, put together nicely
You look good in the moonlight
Hard nipples and your cherry ripe
Tonight, I ain't fucking teasing
I'm doing this for fucking reasons
Baby, you're a mess
I thought it was just me
But you too only want sex
So there's no hesitation
When I start ripping off your dress
I' ma do what I do best
I'll leave your body wrecked
Shaking and dripping
Place my hand upon your neck
Squeezing and nibbling on your nipples
Your special spot is where I'm going to next
I'm simply talking sex
And I'm not saying I'm the best
But I'll make you forget your ex

Move your body like a snake
Slowly in every direction
S&M freaky
Masks and hang cuffs
Strip please
Make me beg, tease
Drive me wild, nuts
Smack my butt
I have fantasies of fucking you on an office desk
I've got the right tools to pick your lock
Get you open off the cock
Leg spread open with me right in between
For you I'm a fiend
You've mastered me, reign supreme
You think of me every time you dream
But we're simply talking sex

Ruff Sex

Ruff sex, bed wet
Now we fucking up the bed set
Ready, set
I 'ma make you sweat
Out your perm
Scream out, tell big daddy what you've learned
I just love to watch you turn
This a workout, won't believe how many calories
I'm gonna make you burn
We're getting nasty
We don't give a fuck about some germs
I'm in control
But don't worry baby I 'ma give you a turn
You gonna taste my sperm
Eww
I said we were going to get nasty
You've got to be careful what you ask me
This ain't about cumming first
It's about how long we last see
Fuck the controversy
It's nap time, welcome to my nursery
You got that ass, eeek
I ain't got time to ask, bee
When you walk past me I've got to be grabby

See you like it from the back
That ass you throw that back
You like when I pull your hair
And my other hand around your neck
See we love fucking
Having sex like it's nothing
You send me a love text
Saying you like it when we do it on our sides
Send tingles right up your spine
From the day we first fucked, I knew your ass was mine

Ruff sex, angry sex
Makeup sex, wakeup sex
Any type of sex
All good because, I get to feel and suck on your breast
Quite tasty, the best
We go for an hour or two
Taking our time, no rush or powering through
I always want you to feel
The full impact of my dick inside of you

Ruff sex
Explicit XX
Let's be specific you screaming out yes, yes!
Now my bedsheets all wet, wet
Scratch my back, tell me you love it just like that
Sex so ruff
Sex so good
We're breaking shit like we're fighting

It's an every night thing
Open your legs, I'm about to dive in
Eat you out like some fried wings
With some nice sauce, damn you got my mind lost
So good, got my eyes cross
How did I get here?
In between your legs, now I'm lost
I've got your time, mind us, the cost?
It seems that's what we do
Every time we get together
It's loud, ruff sex between me and you
The whole time through

Here we go, let me suck on your nipples
Wake up in the morning feeling like a cripple
I know you like it when your hair's pulled
You came for the real shit, ain't down for no bull
Tonight you came hungry, but you're going to leave full
You have a big appetite and I'm a big meal
I'm going to feed you believe me

Yeah, I'm saying what I've got is a big deal
It's going to hurt, so good, girl I'm going to make you squeal
As I turn you out like hot wheels
Get your seatbelt on, you about to ride a roller coaster
I'll roll and post yuh in every position from every poster

To work you out is all I'm wishing to do
I know you've been itching for it too
For me to come and put this dick on you
So tonight let me show you what the business is
You'll feel the differences

We about to fuck
You ain't going to know the difference between me and a fantasy
Take off your panties, for your fan to see
You're already wet, your juice box about to burst
I'm going to work it out until that pussy hurts
You're going to flood the room, as I flood your pum
All of me you're gonna consume
We're about to triple X it
I'm planning to cum in all your exits

Ready for round two of this porn star type shit?
Gotta make room, you got a tight fit
You can't walk, you got that tight shit
No one ever hit that shit like this
Pussy leaking like a faucet
Thinking of me as you take your clothes out the closet
Thinking of me at every step of your day
Remembering those moments I had you losing breath
Running from the D
Saying it's so good "how you're giving it to me"

You play with me in between your jaws
As I play in between your walls
It's my name you're bawling
It's your body that did the calling
Not halfway, baby, I'm all in
Giving you this beautiful pain
Hmm, I think you just came

Hands on the wall, this ain't no ordinary booty call
Facedown, ass arched up
This the type of sex we spark up
I go hard, I'll work you out
Daydreaming of me right after I'm gone

Got you asking yourself questions, you know doubts?
Like "did he really fuck me so good, is he my number one?"
But out goes the doubts when I'm around
Only explicit words coming out of your mouth
When I put it on you,you moan, scream and shout
"ooh, ooh ouch, ouch"
"oh shit, ooh right, ooh fuck me right there, don't stop"
Didn't know sex could be so good laying on a couch
As all your questions I make drift away
Lost in a moment, off-balance we fade away

Tonight there are no limits to the things
I might do in between these sheets
Let me be your bedroom geek
Let me get deeper and deeper
I want to hear your inners speak
I want to hear your pussy preach
Let it sing out my praises
Tongue tornado, to on me you riding
I' ma bring the freak in you out of hiding
Crazy how that shit just tied in
In your pussy, I just dive in
All your wetness I now reside in
Slip and slide
I' ma show you, I' ma different guy
Truth, not a different lie
Consistent with the stroke
Choking, I'm in your throat
You'll have no choice but to give me the title of GOAT
Make you my centrefold and make your center fold
Tomorrow a few stories of this will get told
Tonight let's get bold
Show me, how much of this dick that pussy can hold

Tonight we're acting out our fantasies
An R rated type of love won't do it for me
Tonight we're going to triple X it
No ordinary sex is my guarantee
I plan to have you screaming
"Oh shit, shit!"
'Hmm, right there, that's my spot right there!"
'Hmm, ooh ah Yes!"
'Baby, don't stop! Ah Yes!"
And whenever you think of me
You'll think of sex
Cause I triple X'ed that pussy
Had you dripping wet, wet
Triple X'ed it
Put my name on it so the world knows I sexed it
You won't forget how good I fucked you

Freak Shit (xXx 2

Can I remove your bra and expose your breast
Then with my tongue massage your neck
Then slowly down your body, my lips caress
As my hand squeeze your ass
Nibble on your nipples, suck on them, bite
In between all that I'll throw in a little ice
To cool our fire and make you feel all nice
Work my way down from your upper lips
To the ones on your pussy, give them a kiss

Yes the clitoris
I'm such a gentleman, generous
I'm a freak, for good sex, I'm notorious
But the glory ours
However, the story's just beginning
We won't finish, without a happy ending
Hard dick, wet puss, recommended
You got curves, but I'll make you bend in, ways
You never thought you could
Because of my nicely bent wood
Flip you on your stomach
And then fuck you from the back
Yes just like this
Just to hear you moan
I know you like this
Scream, if you want too
I love your moans
That's a turn on
Got you turned on
Your side, as I rub on your thigh
You love how we fuck
I can tell by the smile on your face and tears in your eyes

Legs wrapped around my waist
Screaming for me not to stop
Pure pleasure, you're about to pop
My dick so hard, you want yourself a taste
All in your mouth and face
My dick in all those out of reach places
Part of the suit of clubs, one of the aces
At least that's what you thought
Don't want this moment to stop
Body boiling over
You like it
Want me to go faster
From day one, I've been your sex master
You're my student, so I gotta teach yuh

Fruits and whip cream involved
Body shaking ignoring all phone calls
You're on an adventure
Fucking in public places
Libraries and bathroom stalls
The backseat of my ride

Discovery, I'll make you find the freak inside
Cameras, that porn star vibe
Breast, ass, lips and vagina
You'll remember me, never need a reminder
The way this dick be inside you
I'll be a permanent fixture in your mind
Fuck lingerie, your skin the perfect design
Fuck Victoria, it's your secrets I want to find
Got you covered in baby oil, got to make that body shine

For your body, I'm a crook, I' ma fiend
Introduced you to things, you had never seen
Steam
Trying to stay dry
Trying to get over all these wet dreams
I'm your everything it seems
Wet, playing for the same teams
Made you squirt
Move, make me work 6 to 9
Eating you out with my dick in your mouth

Ooh
Excuse my language
But this is what fucking is about
What being nasty is about
That freaky shit
That freak me, shit
In and out your mouth and clit
Not wasting an ounce of spit

How Could We Forget

How could we forget?
How we connect
Sweet kisses on your neck
Me squeezing on your leg
In between your pussy is wet
You whisper in my ear
What you want me to do next
Way more than just sex
So quick to undress
Smelling so fresh
Tasting your flesh
So close and attached
Light up, a match
On fire, we gon' catch

How could we forget?
Smooth and direct
Me licking on your kitty
Wanted to be safe
But no safety with me
You have me going in without a hat
That's that
Ass so fat, bouncing off my bat
I love it how you throw that ass back, back
You a cutie, true to type baddie
Instant pics, Polaroid, Kodak
We taking it way, way back
Lingerie see through all black
Like that 90's show
"You all that"
Baby come on over here
Take off all that
Show me what's under there
We've been drinking a little impaired
Hennessey fantasies, we taking part in
Misbehaving, don't beg for pardons
As the night goes on I don't fall off
I bear the burden, my wood stay harden
Don't ever forget
Sweet kisses on your neck
Sweat, wet sheets
You're all out of breath
Never forget how I laid down the pipe
Perfect
Had you bouncing around the room
Like an animal in the circus
I go deep, well below the surface
Never forget
Baby, you know that stress ain't worth it

Yoni-Verse

You told me to enter your yoni-verse
I said baby, you gotta show me your yoni first
Let me get a taste, let the yoni burst
With all of its flavours
I want to be the star that occupies your quasar
Baby surrender, quench your yoni's thirst

Verse
I want to enter your womanhood
You make me feel like no other woman could
Good, stack it
Bring it back in a nice lingerie package
I'll supply the accessories for the adage
You a whole plate, I hope I can manage
I want to treat you right
And lick your body good
If it wasn't me
I know another body could
I don't worry about that
I'll provide that morning and evening wood
And when the yoni starts dripping
Your yoni juice I'll be sipping
Just returning the favour
For you sucking me off before I stuck the tip in

Yeah I talk dirty
I'm a little different
No Metaphors
We can get it on in the back seat of cars
Or on the floor of book stores
I' ma strip you down, and dick you up
If the yoni good I might overact
Hollywood
I likely would
I might get us arrested for public indecency
Got to have it, like a public emergency
Janitor closets
You see the urgency
I'd loved to live inside your yoni-verse
Let me in
Let me get a feel
For what your yoni's worth

www.ingramcontent.com/pod-product-compliance
Lightning Source LLC
Chambersburg PA
CBHW051414250726
48655CB00003B/1038